MIND-B[FACTS
FOR CURIOUS MINDS

EXTRAORDINARY FACTS ABOUT HISTORY SCIENCE, EARTH AND BEYOND TO EXPAND YOUR MIND - SUMMER EDITION

BRIGHT MINDS LEARNING

TABLE OF CONTENTS

INTRODUCTION

Do you have thousands of questions about everything?

Do you like to sound like the smartest one in the room?

When you come across something new, do you get all curious about it and start asking questions like, "How does that even work?"

Do things like celebrating two birthday parties in one day or lighters being invented before matches make you giggle?

If that sounds like you, I've got you covered!

The world is filled with amazing things waiting to be discovered, and every question leads to another exciting adventure!

Summer is the best time for this kind of stuff. You can jump into the mysteries of the world around us. This special summer edition is jam-packed with super fun facts to entertain you all summer.

But wait, there's more! Trivia is a super cool way to break the ice with new friends and challenge your old buds. The awesome facts and quizzes in this book are a fantastic way to kickstart awesome conversations and have a ton of fun. You can quiz each other, learn new things together, and see who can come up with the most mind-blowing facts!

Inside these pages, you will encounter a treasure trove of extraordinary facts about history, science, the Earth, and beyond. Every fact is here to ignite your curiosity and make you go, "Wow!" Plus, there are loads of quizzes to challenge yourself and your friends.

So, grab a seat, get ready to explore, and embark on a super cool summer adventure together. This book is here to help you unravel the world's wonders, one fascinating fact at a time. Have a blast exploring!

EPIC TALES
FROM
THE PAST

TIME TRAVEL TIDBITS

1. During World War II, a dog named Juliana earned a medal for **peeing on a bomb** to put it out!

2. The world's most successful **pirate** in history was a lady named Ching Shih.

3. Napoleon was attacked (and defeated) by a **horde of rabbits.**

4. **Cleopatra** wasn't actually Egyptian!

5. Ketchup was sold in the 1830s as **medicine** to cure upset stomachs!

6. President Zachary Taylor died after eating too **many cherries and drinking milk.**

7. During the Great Depression, people made clothes out of **food sacks.**

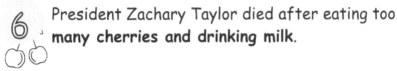

TIME TRAVEL TIDBITS

8 **The shortest war** in history lasted between 38 and 45 minutes!

9 **Tug of War** used to be an Olympic sport!

10 Russia ran out of **vodka** celebrating the end of World War II.

11 Instead of cats, Ancient Romans used **ferrets** to hunt mice and rats.

12 In the 19th century, knocker-uppers were hired by industrial bosses to **wake up** their workers.

13 The **tallest** married couple ever recorded was Anna Haining Swan, who was 7'11", and Martin Van Buren Bates, who was 7'9".

14 The ancient Romans often used stale urine as **mouthwash**.

TIME TRAVEL TIDBITS

15 "**Mary had a little lamb**" was a real 11-year-old girl who lived in Boston and one day was followed to school by her pet lamb!

16 One hundred million years ago, the Sahara Desert was inhabited by galloping **crocodiles**.

17 The South African railway once employed a **baboon** named Jack. He was paid 20 cents a day and half a bottle of beer weekly.

18 The Ancient Egyptians used slabs of stone as **pillows**.

19 **Thomas Edison** didn't invent most of the stuff he patented!

20 Adolf Hitler's **nephew**, William P. Hitler, fought against the Nazis in World War II.

HIDDEN GEMS OF HISTORY

1. THE GREAT PYRAMID OF GIZA

The Great Pyramid of Giza in Egypt is one of the oldest and largest pyramids in the world. It  was built over 4,500 years ago and was originally 481 feet tall. Amazingly, it was the tallest man-made structure in the world for over 3,800 years. It's made of millions of limestone blocks, each weighing as much as 15 tons!

2. THE FIRST OLYMPICS

The first Olympic Games were held in ancient Greece in 776 BC. They were part of a festival to honor the Greek god Zeus. The games included events like running, long jump, shot put, javelin, boxing, and wrestling. Only men could compete, and they did so in the nude!

3. VIKING LONGSHIPS

Vikings were expert sailors and built longships that could travel vast distances across the sea. These ships were fast, flexible, and could even navigate shallow rivers. The Vikings used them to explore, trade, and sometimes raid distant lands. Their ships were a big part of why they were such successful explorers.

4. THE ROMAN COLOSSEUM

The Roman Colosseum is a massive amphitheater in Rome, Italy. It could hold up to 50,000 to 80,000 spectators who came to watch gladiator fights and other public spectacles like animal hunts and mock sea battles. It was built nearly 2,000 years ago and remains one of the greatest architectural achievements of the Roman Empire.

5. THE BLACK DEATH

The Black Death was a devastating plague that swept through Europe in the 14th century. It killed 50 million people, about half of Europe's population. The disease was spread by fleas on rats, and it caused massive social and economic changes. It was one of the deadliest pandemics in human history.

6. LEONARDO DA VINCI

Leonardo da Vinci was a true Renaissance man. He was a painter, scientist, inventor, and more. His famous paintings include the Mona Lisa and The Last Supper. Da Vinci also sketched designs for flying machines, tanks, and other inventions far ahead of his time. He was one of the most brilliant minds in history.

7. THE GREAT WALL OF CHINA

The Great Wall of China is one of the longest structures ever built, stretching over 13,000 miles. It was constructed over many centuries to protect China from invasions. The wall is so long that it could stretch across the United States four times! It's an incredible feat of engineering and human effort.

8. THE FIRST PRINTING PRESS

Johannes Gutenberg invented the first movable type printing press around 1440. This invention made it possible to print books quickly and cheaply, leading to a revolution in the spread of knowledge. The Gutenberg Bible was one of the first major books printed, and it changed the world by making information more accessible.

9. ANCIENT EGYPTIAN HIEROGLYPHS

Ancient Egyptians used a writing system called hieroglyphs, which consisted of pictures and symbols. These were carved into stone or written on papyrus scrolls. The Rosetta Stone, discovered in 1799, helped scholars finally understand and translate these ancient writings. Hieroglyphs give us a glimpse into the lives and beliefs of ancient Egyptians.

10. THE MAGNA CARTA

The Magna Carta was a charter signed by King John of England in 1215. It was one of the first documents to limit a king's power and protect citizens' rights. It laid the groundwork for modern democracy and the rule of law. Many of its principles are still important today.

11. THE INCA EMPIRE

The Inca Empire was the largest empire in pre-Columbian America, stretching along the western coast of South America. The Incas were master builders and engineers, creating amazing structures like Machu Picchu high in the Andes Mountains. They also built extensive road networks and practiced advanced agriculture.

12. THE WRIGHT BROTHERS

In 1903, Orville and Wilbur Wright achieved the first powered flight in a plane called the Wright Flyer. Their flight lasted only 12 seconds and covered 120 feet, but it changed the world forever. The Wright brothers' invention laid the foundation for modern aviation and how we travel today.

13. THE TITANIC

The Titanic was a luxury passenger ship that sank on its maiden voyage in 1912 after hitting an iceberg. Over 1,500 people lost their lives in the disaster. The ship was considered "unsinkable" due to its advanced design. However, the tragedy showed that nature can still overpower human engineering.

14. THE TERRACOTTA ARMY

In China, thousands of life-sized terracotta soldiers were buried with Emperor Qin Shi Huang around 210 BC. These soldiers were meant to protect the emperor in the afterlife. Each statue is unique, with different faces, armor, and weapons. The Terracotta Army is one of the greatest archaeological discoveries ever made.

15. THE MOON LANDING

On July 20, 1969, Neil Armstrong became the first person to walk on the Moon. The Apollo 11 mission was a huge achievement for NASA and space exploration. Armstrong's famous words, "That's one small step for man, one giant leap for mankind," marked an incredible moment in human history.

16. SEVEN WONDERS OF THE ANCIENT WORLD

The Seven Wonders of the Ancient World were incredible structures built by ancient civilizations. They include the Great Pyramid of Giza, the Hanging Gardens of Babylon, the Statue of Zeus at Olympia, the Temple of Artemis at Ephesus, the Mausoleum at Halicarnassus, the Colossus of Rhodes, and the Lighthouse of Alexandria. Each wonder was renowned for its architectural and artistic marvels, and they have fascinated people for thousands of years. The Great Pyramid of Giza is the only one still standing today!

17. THE FIRST HOT AIR BALLOON FLIGHT

In 1783, the first successful hot air balloon flight was made by two French brothers, Joseph-Michel and Jacques-Étienne Montgolfier. They built a large balloon out of silk and paper and heated the air inside with a fire. On its first flight, the balloon carried a sheep, a duck, and a rooster into the sky. Later that same year, the brothers launched the first human passengers, marking the beginning of human flight and paving the way for future aviation adventures!

18. THE UNDERGROUND RAILROAD

The Underground Railroad was a network of secret routes and safe houses used by enslaved African Americans to escape to free states and Canada. Brave people called "conductors," like Harriet Tubman, helped guide the escapees to freedom. It was a dangerous journey, but it led many to a new life away from slavery.

19. THE RENAISSANCE

The Renaissance was a cultural movement that began in Italy in the 14th century and spread across Europe. It was a time of great creativity and learning, with advances in art, science, literature, and philosophy. Famous figures like Leonardo da Vinci, Michelangelo, and Galileo made groundbreaking contributions that still influence us today.

20. THE BERLIN WALL

The Berlin Wall was built in 1961 and separated East and West Berlin in Germany. It was a symbol of the Cold War and divided families and friends for nearly 30 years. In 1989, the wall was finally torn down, leading to the reunification of Germany and the end of the Cold War. The fall of the Berlin Wall is celebrated as a moment of freedom and unity.

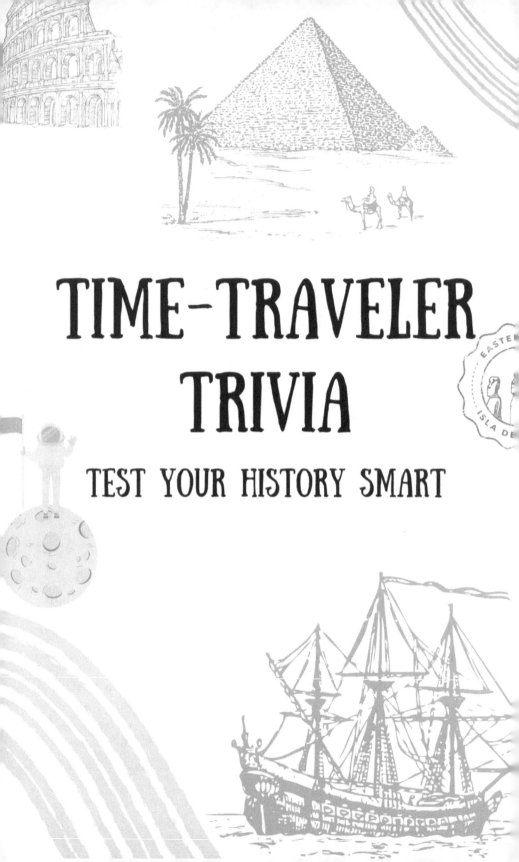

TIME-TRAVELER TRIVIA

TEST YOUR HISTORY SMART

QUIZ 1: ANCIENT EGYPT

Question: What is the purpose of the Great Sphinx of Giza?

A) It was a palace for the pharaoh.

B) It served as a giant sundial.

C) It was built to guard the pyramids.

D) It was used as a granary.

Answer: C) It was built to guard the pyramids.

The Great Sphinx of Giza is a massive statue with the body of a lion and the head of a pharaoh. It was built to guard the pyramids and serve as a symbol of strength and wisdom. The Sphinx is one of the most iconic monuments of ancient Egypt and stands near the Great Pyramid of Giza. It's carved out of limestone and is about 240 feet long and 66 feet tall, making it an impressive sight to behold.

QUIZ 2: ROMAN EMPIRE

Question: Who was the first emperor of Rome?

A) Julius Caesar

B) Augustus

C) Nero

D) Hadrian

Answer: B) Augustus.

Augustus, originally named Octavian, was the first emperor of Rome. He came to power after the assassination of his great-uncle Julius Caesar and established the Roman Empire in 27 BCE. Augustus ruled for over 40 years, bringing peace and stability to the region.

QUIZ 3: THE MIDDLE AGES

Question: What was a knight's primary duty during the Middle Ages?

A) Farming the land.

B) Serving in the army.

C) Writing books.

D) Making clothes.

Answer: B) Serving in the army.

Knights were warriors in the Middle Ages who served as soldiers for their lords and kings. They were trained in combat and followed a code of chivalry, which emphasized bravery, honor, and respect for women and the weak. Knights often participated in battles and tournaments.

QUIZ 4: MEDIEVAL TIMES

Question: What was the primary purpose of a castle in medieval times?

A) To serve as a marketplace.

B) To provide entertainment.

C) To defend and protect the inhabitants.

D) To grow crops.

Answer: C) To defend and protect the inhabitants.

Castles were built primarily for defense and protection during medieval times. They were fortified structures that served as residences for nobles and their families, and as strongholds to protect against enemy attacks. Castles often had thick walls, moats, and towers to enhance their defensive capabilities.

QUIZ 5: AMERICAN REVOLUTION

Question: Who was the main author of the Declaration of Independence?

A) George Washington

B) Benjamin Franklin

C) Thomas Jefferson

D) John Adams

Answer: C) Thomas Jefferson.

Thomas Jefferson was the primary author of the Declaration of Independence, which was adopted on July 4, 1776. This historic document declared the American colonies' independence from British rule and outlined the principles of individual liberty and government by consent.

QUIZ 6: ANCIENT CHINESE INVENTIONS

Question: Which ancient Chinese invention was originally used for fireworks and later for weapons?

A) Compass

B) Gunpowder

C) Paper

D) Silk

Answer: B) Gunpowder.

Gunpowder was invented in ancient China during the Tang dynasty (618-907 AD). It was originally used to create fireworks to celebrate events and ward off evil spirits. Later, the Chinese discovered that gunpowder could be used in weapons such as bombs, cannons, and guns. This invention had a profound impact on warfare and spread to other parts of the world, changing the course of history.

QUIZ 7: FAMOUS EXPLORERS

Question: Who was the first explorer to circumnavigate the globe?

A) Christopher Columbus

B) Ferdinand Magellan

C) Marco Polo

D) Vasco da Gama

Answer: B) Ferdinand Magellan.

Ferdinand Magellan, a Portuguese explorer, led the first expedition to circumnavigate the globe from 1519 to 1522. Although Magellan was killed during the journey, his expedition completed the voyage, proving that the Earth is round and that it is possible to sail around it.

QUIZ 8: THE INDUSTRIAL REVOLUTION

Question: What invention is James Watt famous for improving?

A) The printing press

B) The steam engine

C) The telephone

D) The light bulb

Answer: B) The steam engine.

James Watt significantly improved the steam engine in the late 18th century, making it more efficient and practical for use in industry and transportation. His enhancements helped drive the Industrial Revolution, leading to advancements in manufacturing, mining, and the development of steam-powered trains and ships.

QUIZ 9: THE INDUSTRIAL REVOLUTION (PART 2)

Question: Which invention is credited with starting the Industrial Revolution by greatly improving the efficiency of textile production?

A) Steam engine

B) Cotton gin

C) Spinning jenny

D) Telegraph

Answer: C) Spinning jenny.

The spinning jenny, invented by James Hargreaves in 1764, revolutionized textile production by allowing one worker to spin multiple threads at once. This greatly increased the efficiency and speed of making yarn, leading to significant advancements in the textile industry and helping to kickstart the Industrial Revolution.

QUIZ 10: THE AMERICAN CIVIL WAR

Question: Who was the president of the United States during the Civil War?

A) Thomas Jefferson

B) Abraham Lincoln

C) George Washington

D) Theodore Roosevelt

Answer: B) Abraham Lincoln.

Abraham Lincoln was the president of the United States during the Civil War, which lasted from 1861 to 1865. He is best known for his leadership during the war, his efforts to end slavery, and his famous Gettysburg Address. Lincoln's Emancipation Proclamation declared all slaves in Confederate-held territory free.

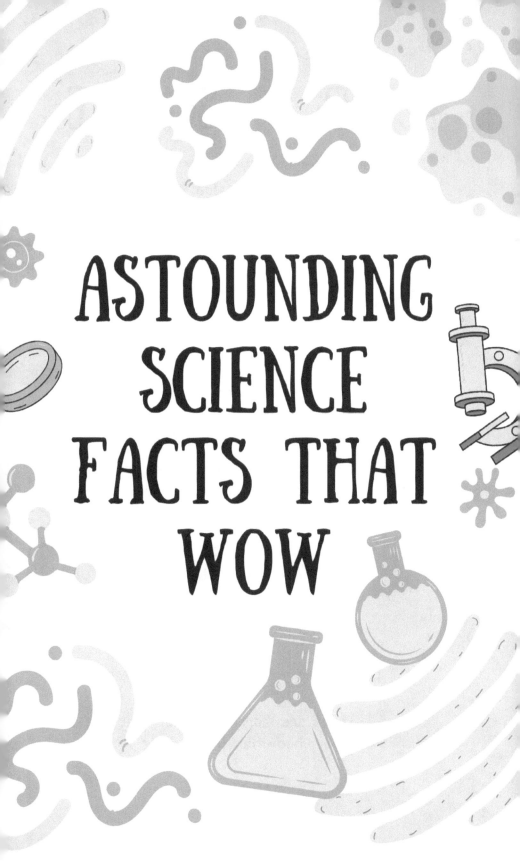

ASTOUNDING SCIENCE FACTS THAT WOW

A BITE OF SCIENCE

1
A **single cloud** can weigh as much as a million pounds, which is like having 100 elephants floating in the sky!

2
Only **female** mosquitoes drink blood as a protein source for their eggs.

3
Your **brain** is constantly eating itself.

4
In 1945, a chicken named Mike lived for an incredible **18 months** without a head!

5
In the real world, there's no such thing as a **perfectly straight line** or a **perfect circle**.

6 **Lighters** were invented before matches!

7
There are more **bacterial cells** in your body than human cells.

A BITE OF SCIENCE

8 Animals can be **allergic** to humans' dead skin cells.

9 Peanut butter can be converted into **diamonds** by subjecting it to extremely high temperatures and pressure.

10 One **lightning bolt** could cook 20,000 pieces of toast.

11 You remember more **dreams** when you sleep badly.

12 The longest anyone has held their breath **underwater** is 24 minutes and 37 seconds.

13 **Flamingos** get their pink color from their food.

14 You can't fold a piece of A4 paper more than **eight** times.

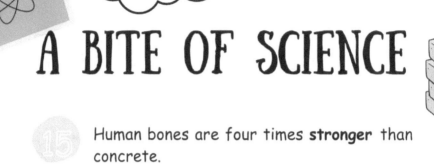

A BITE OF SCIENCE

15 Human bones are four times **stronger** than concrete.

16 Hot water **freezes** faster than cold water.

17 Identical **twins** don't have the same fingerprints.

18 The majority of Earth's oxygen is produced by plant-based marine organisms from **oceans**.

19 Bananas are **radioactive**.

20 Without **saliva**, you cannot taste anything.

A FEAST OF SCIENCE FACTS

1. LIGHTNING STRIKES

Did you know that a single bolt of lightning can heat the air around it to five times hotter than the surface of the Sun? That's super hot, reaching temperatures of up to 50,000 degrees Fahrenheit! Lightning strikes can also be incredibly powerful, with enough energy to light up a small city. It's a dazzling and dangerous natural phenomenon.

2. JELLYFISH IN SPACE

In 1991, jellyfish were sent to space to see how they react to zero gravity. They multiplied in space like on Earth, but when they returned, they had trouble adjusting to gravity. The jellyfish struggled to swim properly, showing how different life can be without Earth's gravitational pull. This experiment helped scientists understand more about living in space.

3. RAINBOWS AT NIGHT

Rainbows can happen at night, and they're called moonbows! They are created by the light of the Moon, just like rainbows are created by sunlight. Moonbows are usually very faint and appear white because the Moon's light is not as strong as the Sun's. They are a rare and beautiful sight to behold.

4. WALKING ON AIR

Thanks to millions of tiny hairs on their feet, geckos can walk on walls and even upside down. These hairs, called setae, stick to surfaces using a special electrical attraction called van der Waals forces. This amazing ability allows geckos to escape predators and hunt for food in tricky places. They are true acrobats of the animal world!

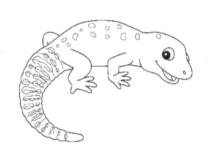

5. WATER'S AMAZING TRICKS

Water is the only substance on Earth that can naturally exist in three forms: solid (ice), liquid (water), and gas (steam). This unique property of water is due to its molecular structure, allowing it to easily change states with temperature changes. It plays a vital role in our daily lives and the environment. From glaciers to clouds, water is everywhere!

6. DEEPEST POINT ON EARTH

The Mariana Trench in the Pacific Ocean is the deepest point on Earth, reaching about 36,000 feet deep. That's like stacking almost 25 Empire State Buildings on each other! The pressure at the bottom is so intense that it's like having the weight of 100 adult elephants pressing down on you. It's a dark, mysterious world that we're still exploring.

7. THE INVISIBLE SHIELD

Earth has an invisible shield called the magnetosphere that protects us from harmful solar wind and cosmic rays. This magnetic field is generated by the movement of molten iron in Earth's outer core. Without it, our atmosphere could be stripped away, and life as we know it wouldn't exist. It's a powerful force field that keeps us safe every day.

8. SPINNING EARTH

Earth spins at about 1,000 miles per hour, but you don't feel it because everything around you, including the air, is spinning with you. This spinning motion gives us day and night as different parts of the Earth face the Sun. It's also why we have different time zones across the world. The Earth's spin is like a giant merry-go-round that never stops!

9. SMELLY SKUNK

Adult skunks can spray their stinky smell up to 10 feet away accurately, but with the help of wind, the spray can go to 20 feet. The scent is so strong that a human nose can detect it from at least a mile and a half away! This smelly spray is produced by glands under their tails and is used to scare off predators. Skunks are like little stink bombs, ready to go off if they feel threatened.

10. THE POWER OF THE SUN

Every second, the Sun produces enough energy to power the entire Earth for 500,000 years! This enormous energy comes from nuclear reactions happening at the Sun's core, where hydrogen atoms fuse to form helium. The Sun's energy supports all life on Earth by providing light and warmth. It's a gigantic powerhouse in the sky.

11. GIANT SEQUOIA TREES

The giant sequoia trees are some of the largest living things on Earth. One tree, named General Sherman, is over 275 feet tall and weighs about 2.7 million pounds! These ancient trees can live for more than 3,000 years, surviving fires and harsh weather. Visiting a sequoia forest is like stepping into a land of giants.

12. FASTEST WIND ON NEPTUNE

The wind on Neptune can blow as fast as 1,200 miles per hour, which is faster than the speed of sound! These powerful winds create huge storms that can last for years. Neptune's atmosphere is made mostly of hydrogen, helium, and methane, which gives the planet its beautiful blue color. It's a windy and wild world far from Earth.

13. ELECTRIFYING EELS

Electric eels can produce electric shocks of up to 600 volts to stun prey and defend themselves. That's enough electricity to light up ten light bulbs! They use special organs in their bodies to generate these shocks. Electric eels live in the murky waters of South America and are like underwater superheroes with their shocking powers.

14. COOL PENGUINS

Penguins have a special gland above their eyes that removes salt from the seawater they drink. This keeps them hydrated even in salty oceans. Penguins also have thick layers of blubber and feathers to keep them warm in freezing temperatures. These fascinating birds are excellent swimmers and can dive deep into the ocean for food.

15. THE OLDEST LIVING THING

The oldest known living organism is a type of sea sponge called the glass sponge. Some of these sponges have lived in the deep sea for over 10,000 years! They thrive in the cold, dark waters and grow very slowly.

16. GROWING BAMBOO

Bamboo is the fastest-growing plant in the world. It can grow up to 35 inches in a single day, which is about 1.5 inches per hour! This rapid growth makes bamboo a great resource for building materials and products. It's also a favorite food of pandas, who rely on bamboo forests for their diet.

17. INVISIBLE FROGS

Some frogs in the rainforest are transparent, meaning you can see their hearts beating and their stomachs digesting food right through their skin. These glass frogs use their see-through bodies to hide from predators. Their unique camouflage makes them one of nature's coolest hide-and-seek champions.

18. AMAZING HONEY

Honey never spoils, and archaeologists have found pots of honey in ancient Egyptian tombs that are over 3,000 years old and still perfectly edible. Honey's long shelf life is due to its low moisture content and acidic pH, which make it hard for bacteria to grow. It's a sweet treat that lasts forever!

19. TWINKLING STARS

Stars twinkle because their light has to pass through Earth's atmosphere. The atmosphere's moving air bends the starlight, making the stars appear to twinkle. This shimmering effect is more noticeable with stars closer to the horizon. Next time you see a twinkling star, you'll know it's because of the air we're breathing!

20. DINOSAUR FEATHERS

Some dinosaurs had feathers! Scientists think that feathers might have been used for warmth, display, and eventually for flight in some species. Discoveries of feathered dinosaur fossils have changed our understanding of how these ancient creatures looked and lived. Imagine a T-rex with feathers - how cool is that?

SCIENCE TRIVIA FOR GENIUSES

QUIZ 1: THE MAGIC OF MAGNETISM

Question: What happens if you put the north pole of one magnet near the south pole of another magnet?

A) They repel each other.

B) They attract each other.

C) Nothing happens.

D) They make a loud noise.

Answer: B) They attract each other.

Opposite poles of magnets attract each other, which means the north pole of one magnet will pull towards the south pole of another. This happens because magnetic fields interact in such a way that opposite poles pull together. This attraction is what makes magnets stick to each other or to metal objects like the fridge door!

QUIZ 2: FUN WITH FROGS

Question: How do frogs breathe?

A) Through their skin.

B) Through their lungs.

C) Through gills.

D) All of the above.

Answer: D) All of the above.

Frogs are amazing creatures that can breathe in different ways throughout their lives. Like fish, tadpoles use gills to breathe underwater. As they grow into adult frogs, they develop lungs for breathing air. Additionally, adult frogs can absorb oxygen directly through their moist skin, especially when they are in water. This makes them well-adapted to living both in water and on land.

QUIZ 3: THE WONDERS OF WATER

Question: What percentage of the human body is made up of water?

A) 30%

B) 50%

C) 60%

D) 90%

Answer: C) 60%.

Around 60% of the human body is composed of water. This vital liquid is found in every cell, tissue, and organ in our bodies, helping to regulate temperature, transport nutrients, and remove waste. Water is essential for digestion, circulation, and even for our brains to function properly. Staying hydrated is key to keeping our bodies healthy and active.

QUIZ 4: SOLAR SYSTEM SPIN

Question: Which planet spins the fastest on its axis?

A) Earth

B) Mars

C) Jupiter

D) Venus

Answer: C) Jupiter.

Jupiter is the fastest-spinning planet in our solar system. It completes one rotation in just about 10 hours. This rapid spin creates very strong winds and massive storms, including the Great Red Spot, which is a giant storm that has been raging for centuries. Even though Jupiter is a huge gas giant, its quick rotation causes it to bulge out at the equator and flatten at the poles.

QUIZ 5: PLANT POWER

Question: What part of the plant conducts photosynthesis?

A) Roots

B) Stem

C) Leaves

D) Flowers

Answer: C) Leaves.

Photosynthesis takes place in the leaves of plants. Leaves contain chlorophyll, a green pigment that captures sunlight. During photosynthesis, plants use sunlight, water, and carbon dioxide to create food in the form of glucose and release oxygen as a byproduct. This process not only feeds the plant but also provides oxygen for us to breathe.

QUIZ 6: DIGGING INTO DINOSAURS

Question: What does the word "dinosaur" mean?

A) Huge lizard

B) Terrible lizard

C) Ancient reptile

D) Giant beast

Answer: B) Terrible lizard.

The word "dinosaur" comes from the Greek words "deinos," meaning terrible, and "sauros," meaning lizard. This name was chosen because early fossil discoveries suggested these creatures were enormous and fearsome. Dinosaurs roamed the Earth millions of years ago and came in all shapes and sizes, from the tiny Compsognathus to the massive Argentinosaurus.

QUIZ 7: SOUNDS IN SPACE

Question: Can sound travel in space?

A) Yes, it travels faster.

B) No, there's no air.

C) Yes, but only certain sounds.

D) No, it's too dark.

Answer: B) No, there's no air.

Sound needs a medium like air, water, or solid materials to travel through. Space is a vacuum, meaning it has no air or any other medium to carry sound waves. That's why astronauts use radios to communicate with each other in space. Without air, sound waves have no way to travel, making space completely silent.

QUIZ 8: ELECTRIFYING KNOWLEDGE

Question: What natural phenomenon is the result of static electricity in the atmosphere?

A) Rain

B) Snow

C) Lightning

D) Wind

Answer: C) Lightning.

Lightning is a giant spark of electricity that occurs in the atmosphere. It happens when there is a buildup of static electricity in storm clouds. When the electrical charge becomes too great, it is released in a flash of lightning. This powerful discharge can light up the sky and is often followed by the sound of thunder as the air rapidly expands and contracts.

QUIZ 9: DEEP SEA MYSTERIES

Question: Which is the largest animal in the ocean?

A) Great white shark

B) Giant squid

C) Blue whale

D) Orca

Answer: C) Blue whale.

The blue whale is the largest animal to have ever lived on Earth. These gentle giants can grow up to 100 feet long and weigh as much as 200 tons. Despite their massive size, blue whales feed on tiny shrimp-like creatures called krill. They can consume up to 4 tons of krill each day during feeding season!

QUIZ 10: AMAZING ANATOMY

Question: What is the strongest muscle in the human body relative to its size?

A) Biceps

B) Heart

C) Tongue

D) Jaw muscle (masseter)

Answer: D) Jaw muscle (masseter).

The masseter muscle, located in the jaw, is the strongest muscle in the human body relative to its size. It allows you to chew and can generate a powerful bite force. This muscle can apply significant pressure, enabling you to chew tough foods like nuts and meat. The masseter's strength is vital for eating and speaking.

OUT-OF-THE-WORLD
FACTS ABOUT
EARTH

A PEAK OF EARTH'S SECRETS

1. Only 1% of all the water on Earth is **drinkable**.

2. In Death Valley, some rocks seem to "**walk**" on their own, leaving trails behind them thanks to ice and wind!

3. There are about **6,000 lightning strikes** every minute, which is more than 8 million strikes every day.

4. In the center of the Atacama Desert, there are places where rain has **never** been recorded.

5. In Switzerland, it is **illegal** to own just one guinea pig because they need companionship.

6. The Earth's longest mountain range is **underwater**!

A PEAK OF EARTH'S SECRETS

North Pole

7. Earth's magnetic **North Pole** moves in loops of up to 50 miles (80 km) per day.

8. The Greek name for Earth was **Gaia**. It means "Mother Earth."

9. Earth is home to **8.7 million** different species of plants and animals!

10. Stromboli volcano has been erupting off and on for about **2,000 years**.

11. Earth is the only planet that is not named after a **Greek or Roman god**.

12. Only **5%** of the ocean has been explored.

13. Saint Lucia is the only country in the world named after a **woman**.

A PEAK OF EARTH'S SECRETS

14 The national animal of Scotland is a **unicorn**.

15 The Antarctic desert is the largest in the world, **double** the size of the Sahara Desert.

16 The Earth is the only place in our solar system where a **Solar Eclipse** can happen.

17 Antarctica wasn't covered in ice for more than **100 million years**.

18 The Himalayas are the **highest** mountain range in the world, home to the ten tallest peaks on Earth.

19 **Mount Thor** has the greatest vertical drop on Earth (4,101 feet).

20 The **Philippines** has an island in a lake on an island in a lake on an island.

UNVEILING EARTH'S MYSTERIES

1. EARTH'S AGE

Earth is about 4.5 billion years old. It formed from a cloud of gas and dust left over from the birth of the Sun. Over billions of years, Earth has changed a lot, from a hot, molten rock to the beautiful blue and green planet we live on today.

2. THE BLUE PLANET

About 71% of Earth's surface is covered in water, which is why it's often called the Blue Planet. Most of this water is in the oceans, but there's also water in rivers, lakes, glaciers, and underground. Water is essential for all known forms of life.

3. TALLEST MOUNTAIN

Mount Everest is the tallest mountain on Earth, standing at 29,032 feet above sea level. Located in the Himalayas, it's so tall that climbers need oxygen tanks to reach the summit because the air is so thin at that height.

4. THE TALLEST WATERFALL

Angel Falls is the tallest waterfall in the world. It has an incredible height of 3,212 feet, with a continuous drop of 2,648 feet. That's so tall that water turns into mist before it reaches the ground!

5. EARTH'S LAYERS

Earth has four main layers: the crust, the mantle, the outer core, and the inner core. The crust is where we live, the mantle is a semi-solid rock that moves slowly, and the core is made mostly of iron and nickel, with the outer core being liquid and the inner core solid.

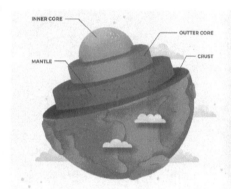

6. LARGEST HOT DESERT

The Sahara Desert in Africa is the largest hot desert in the world, covering about 3.6 million square miles. It's nearly the size of the United States! Despite its harsh conditions, many plants and animals have adapted to live there.

7. THE ATMOSPHERE

Earth's atmosphere is a layer of gases that surrounds our planet and is crucial for life. It protects us from harmful solar radiation, keeps temperatures stable, and contains the oxygen we breathe. The atmosphere is made up of layers. Moving upward from ground level, they include the troposphere, stratosphere, mesosphere, thermosphere, and exosphere. We humans live in the troposphere, and nearly all weather occurs in this lowest layer.

8. EARTH'S ORBIT

Earth orbits the Sun at an average distance of about 93 million miles. It takes 365.25 days to complete one orbit, which is why we have leap years every four years to keep our calendar in sync with Earth's journey around the Sun.

9. PLATE TECTONICS

Earth's crust is divided into huge plates that float on the semi-liquid mantle below. These plates move very slowly, but their movement causes earthquakes, volcanic eruptions, and the formation of mountains. This process is known as plate tectonics.

10. THE NORTHERN LIGHTS

The Northern Lights, or Aurora Borealis, are a spectacular light show in the sky near the North Pole. They are caused by charged particles from the Sun interacting with Earth's magnetic field and atmosphere. The result is beautiful, dancing lights in green, pink, and purple.

11. EARTH'S OLDEST TREE

The oldest known tree in the world is a Bristlecone Pine named Methuselah, located in California's White Mountains.

Methuselah is over 4,800 years old, which means it was already ancient when the pyramids were being built in Egypt! These trees are incredibly resilient and can live in harsh conditions for thousands of years.

12. VOLCANOES

There are about 1,500 active volcanoes on Earth. Volcanoes form when magma from the mantle reaches the surface. When they erupt, they can create new landforms, spew ash into the atmosphere, and even affect the climate.

13. GRAVITY

Gravity is the force that pulls objects toward the center of the Earth. It keeps everything from floating away and gives us weight. Without gravity, we wouldn't be able to walk, plants wouldn't grow upright, and the oceans would float away into space.

14. THE WATER CYCLE

Did you know that the water you drink today could be the same water that dinosaurs drank millions of years ago? Thanks to the water cycle, Earth's water is constantly being recycled. The water you see in rivers, lakes, and even the water in your glass has been around for billions of years, traveling through evaporation, condensation, and precipitation over and over again. So, every time you take a sip, you're tasting a bit of ancient history!

15. THE BLUE HOLE

The Great Blue Hole is a giant marine sinkhole off the coast of Belize. It's over 300 meters (984 feet) across and about 125 meters (410 feet) deep. This deep blue circle is a popular spot for divers and is home to unique marine life. The Great Blue Hole was formed during several episodes of glaciation when sea levels were much lower.

16. EARTH'S SEASONS

Earth's seasons are caused by the planet's tilt. Earth is tilted at an angle of about 23.5 degrees on its axis. This means that as Earth orbits the Sun, different parts of the planet get more direct sunlight at other times of the year. When the Northern Hemisphere is tilted towards the Sun, it experiences summer, while the Southern Hemisphere has winter.

Six months later, the situation is reversed! This tilt is why we have seasons like spring, summer, autumn, and winter. So next time you enjoy a sunny summer day or a snowy winter scene, you can thank Earth's tilt!

17. THE RING OF FIRE

The Ring of Fire is a 25,000-mile horseshoe-shaped zone around the edges of the Pacific Ocean where many earthquakes and volcanic eruptions occur. It's home to about 75% of the world's active volcanoes. This area is very geologically active because of the movement of tectonic plates.

18. EARTHQUAKES

The Great Chilean Earthquake of 1960 had a magnitude of 9.5, making it the most powerful earthquake in history. It was so intense that it actually caused the Earth to wobble slightly on its axis, shortening the length of a day by a few milliseconds! This massive quake also generated tsunamis that traveled across the Pacific Ocean, affecting countries as far away as Japan and the Philippines.

19. GLACIERS

A glacier is a huge mass of ice that moves slowly over land. The term "glacier" comes from the French word glace (glah-SAY), which means ice. Glaciers are often called "rivers of ice.". They store about 69% of the world's fresh water. Glaciers shape landscapes by carving valleys and moving rocks. When they melt, they contribute to rising sea levels.

20. SAND SWIMMING POOLS

Did you know that the Sahara Desert, the largest hot desert in the world, is covered with enough sand to fill millions of Olympic-sized swimming pools? The Sahara spans about 3.6 million square miles, and its sand dunes can reach heights of up to 600 feet!

Even though the Sahara is one of the driest places on Earth, it's home to a variety of plants and animals that have adapted to the harsh environment. And here's another fun fact: the sand in deserts like the Sahara constantly moves and reshapes due to the wind, creating ever-changing landscapes!

EARTH TRIVIA
CHALLENGE

QUIZ 1: VOLCANIC POWER

Question: Which volcano is the tallest above sea level?

A) Mount St. Helens

B) Mount Etna

C) Mount Fuji

D) Mauna Kea

Answer: D) Mauna Kea.

Mauna Kea, located in Hawaii, is the tallest volcano above sea level. When measured from its base on the ocean floor, it is over 33,000 feet tall, making it taller than Mount Everest! Mauna Kea is a dormant volcano and is also home to some of the world's most important astronomical observatories.

QUIZ 2: EARTH'S CHANGING DAYS

Question: Why are the days on Earth gradually getting longer over time?

A) The Earth is spinning faster.

B) The Earth is moving closer to the Sun.

C) The Moon's gravitational pull is slowing down Earth's rotation.

D) The Earth's axis is tilting more.

Answer: C) The Moon's gravitational pull is slowing down Earth's rotation.

The days on Earth are gradually getting longer because the Moon's gravitational pull creates tidal forces that slow down Earth's rotation. This effect causes the length of a day to increase by about 1.7 milliseconds per century. Over millions of years, this gradual slowing will make the days even longer!

QUIZ 3: EARTH'S ATMOSPHERE

Question: Which gas makes up the largest part of the Earth's atmosphere?

A) Oxygen

B) Nitrogen

C) Carbon Dioxide

D) Hydrogen

Answer: B) Nitrogen.

About 78% of the Earth's atmosphere is made up of nitrogen. Oxygen makes up around 21%, and the remaining 1% consists of other gases like argon, carbon dioxide, and small amounts of different gases. The atmosphere is crucial for supporting life, providing oxygen for us to breathe and protecting us from harmful solar radiation.

QUIZ 4: EARTH'S CONTINENTS

Question: What was the name of the supercontinent that existed when all the continents were joined together?

A) Gondwana

B) Pangaea

C) Laurasia

D) Atlantis

Answer: B) Pangaea.

About 300 million years ago, all the Earth's continents were joined together in a single massive supercontinent called Pangaea. Over millions of years, the tectonic plates slowly moved apart due to the process of continental drift, eventually forming the separate continents we know today. This movement is still happening, and the continents continue to shift a few centimeters each year.

QUIZ 5: THE ROCK CYCLE

Question: Which type of rock is formed from cooled lava or magma?

A) Sedimentary rock

B) Metamorphic rock

C) Igneous rock

D) Fossil rock

Answer: C) Igneous rock.

Ignerous Rock

Igneous rocks are formed when lava or magma cools and solidifies. If the magma cools slowly beneath the Earth's surface, it forms intrusive igneous rocks with large crystals, like granite. If the lava cools quickly on the surface, it forms extrusive igneous rocks with small crystals, like basalt.

QUIZ 6: EARTH'S OCEANS

Question: What is the largest ocean on Earth?

A) Atlantic Ocean

B) Indian Ocean

C) Arctic Ocean

D) Pacific Ocean

Answer: D) Pacific Ocean.

The Pacific Ocean is the largest and deepest ocean on Earth, covering more than 63 million square miles. It stretches from the west coast of the Americas to the east coast of Asia and Australia. The Pacific Ocean is so vast that it contains more than half of the world's ocean water.

QUIZ 7: WEATHER PHENOMENA

Question: What does the phrase "the calm before the storm" refer to in weather?

A) The beginning of a storm.

B) The clear and quiet weather that often occurs just before a storm arrives.

C) The eye of the storm.

D) The end of a storm.

Answer: B) The clear and quiet weather that often occurs just before a storm arrives.

The phrase "the calm before the storm" refers to the period of clear and quiet weather that often occurs just before a storm hits. During this time, the atmosphere can become unusually still and peaceful. This calmness happens because the storm system's pressure changes can temporarily stabilize the weather, creating a deceptive sense of tranquility right before the storm's intensity arrives.

QUIZ 8: EXPLODING LAKES

Question: Which phenomenon can cause a lake to explode?

A) Earthquake

B) Volcanic eruption

C) Limnic eruption

D) Tsunami

Answer: C) Limnic eruption.

A limnic eruption, also known as a "lake overturn," is a rare and fascinating phenomenon where dissolved carbon dioxide (CO_2) suddenly erupts from deep lake waters. This can cause the lake to "explode," releasing a large cloud of CO_2 gas that can be deadly to nearby wildlife and humans. One of the most famous instances occurred at Lake Nyos in Cameroon in 1986, where a limnic eruption released a massive cloud of CO_2, resulting in the tragic loss of nearly 1,800 lives. This rare natural disaster is a stark reminder of the dynamic and sometimes dangerous nature of our planet's water bodies.

QUIZ 9: EARTH'S GEOGRAPHY

Question: What is the lowest point on land?

A) Death Valley

B) Mariana Trench

C) Dead Sea

D) Grand Canyon

Answer: C) Dead Sea.

The Dead Sea is the lowest point on land, sitting about 430 meters (1,411 feet) below sea level. Located between Jordan and Israel, the Dead Sea is famous for its extremely salty water, which allows people to float effortlessly. The high salinity also means that very few organisms can live in it, hence its name. This unique body of water is not only a geographical marvel but also a popular destination for its buoyant waters and therapeutic mud.

QUIZ 10: EARTH'S RESOURCES

Question: Which of the following is a renewable resource?

A) Coal

B) Oil

C) Wind

D) Natural gas

Answer: C) Wind.

Wind is a renewable resource because it can be used to generate energy without depleting it. Wind turbines convert the kinetic energy of wind into electricity. Unlike fossil fuels such as coal, oil, and natural gas, which can take millions of years to form, wind is constantly replenished by natural processes in the Earth's atmosphere.

AMAZING NATURE FACTS

WILD AND WACKY NATURE

1. You are always looking at your nose, but your brain chooses to **ignore** it.

2. Snails have **thousands** of teeth.

3. Hippos create a thick, oily, red-colored liquid that acts like natural **sunscreen**.

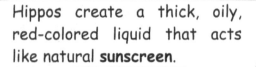

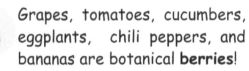

4. Butterflies taste food with their **feet**!

5. Grapes, tomatoes, cucumbers, eggplants, chili peppers, and bananas are botanical **berries**!

6. You get goosebumps when you're scared to make yourself look **bigger**.

7. Bananas are curved because they grow **towards** the Sun.

WILD AND WACKY NATURE

8 During your lifetime, you will produce enough saliva to fill **50 bathtubs**!

9 **Bees** can recognize faces, and they even do it the same way we do.

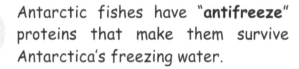

10 Antarctic fishes have "**antifreeze**" proteins that make them survive Antarctica's freezing water.

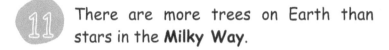

11 There are more trees on Earth than stars in the **Milky Way**.

12 Pineapples take **two years** to grow and have their first fruit.

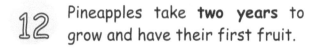

13 **Clownfish** all start their lives as males, but as they grow older, they become female.

14 **Octopuses** have blue blood, three hearts, and a doughnut-shaped brain.

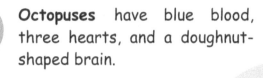

WILD AND WACKY NATURE

15 **Gentoo penguins** give one another stones to show their love.

16 The loudest animal on Earth is a **shrimp**.

17 Some **sharks** can identify blood a quarter-mile away.

18 The water skipper's legs are so buoyant they can support **fifteen times** its weight without sinking.

19 Strawberries are the only fruit that wears their seeds on the **outside**.

20 An average-sized California redwood tree can provide enough wood to make **170,100 pencils**.

EPIC ENCOUNTERS WITH NATURE

1. BUTTERFLY MIGRATION

Every year, millions of monarch butterflies journey from Canada and the United States all the way to Mexico for the winter. They travel in huge groups and use the Sun and Earth's magnetic field to navigate. This incredible trip can be up to 3,000 miles long! What's even more amazing is that the butterflies that start the journey are not the same ones that finish it; it takes several generations of monarchs to complete the round trip.

2. CORAL REEFS

Coral reefs are underwater cities made of tiny animals called coral polyps. They are home to thousands of fish and other creatures. Coral reefs are often called the rainforests of the sea because of their incredible biodiversity.

3. CAMOUFLAGE

The mimic octopus can change its shape, color, and behavior to imitate other sea creatures. This incredible octopus, found in the waters of Southeast Asia, can transform to look like a lionfish, a flatfish, or even a sea snake! It uses this amazing ability to hide from predators and sneak up on prey. Its incredible camouflage skills make it one of the ocean's ultimate masters of disguise!

4. POLLINATION

Bees, butterflies, birds, and even bats help plants reproduce by transferring pollen from one flower to another. This process, called pollination, is essential for plants to produce seeds and fruit. About one out of every three bites of food we eat depends on pollinators.

5. BIOLUMINESCENCE

Did you know that some animals can glow in the dark? Creatures like fireflies, certain types of jellyfish, and deep-sea fish have a special ability called bioluminescence, which allows them to produce their own light. They use this amazing glow to attract mates, lure prey, or scare off predators.

6. HUMMINGBIRDS

Hummingbirds are tiny birds with incredible abilities. They can hover in mid-air by flapping their wings up to 80 times per second, and they can even fly backwards! Despite their small size, hummingbirds have a huge appetite, eating up to twice their body weight in nectar and insects each day. Their fast metabolism and rapid wing beats make them one of nature's most fascinating flyers.

7. THE AMAZON RAINFOREST

The Amazon Rainforest, often called the "lungs of the Earth," produces about 20% of the world's oxygen. It's the largest tropical rainforest, covering over 2.1 million square miles in South America. The Amazon is home to an incredible variety of plants and animals, many of which are found nowhere else on Earth.

8. THE WOOD WIDE WEB

Trees in a forest are connected through an underground network of fungi called mycorrhizae, often referred to as the "Wood Wide Web." This network allows trees to share nutrients, send warnings about pests, and help each other grow. For example, if one tree is attacked by insects, it can send chemical signals through the network to warn nearby trees, which then produce chemicals to defend themselves. It's like trees have their own secret way of talking and helping each other out!

9. ARCTIC FOXES

Arctic foxes change their fur color with the seasons to stay hidden from predators and sneak up on prey. In the winter, their fur turns white to blend in with the snow, providing perfect camouflage against the icy landscape. When summer arrives and the snow melts, their fur changes to a brown or gray color, matching the rocks and plants of the tundra.

10. ELEPHANTS

Elephants can remember the locations of watering holes, food sources, and migration routes even after many years. They can also recognize other elephants and humans they've met before, even after a long time apart. An elephant's strong memory helps them survive in the wild, navigate their vast habitats, and maintain social bonds with their herd. These gentle giants truly have incredible brains!

11. WONDERFUL TRAVELERS

Did you know that plants have clever ways to spread their seeds far and wide? Some seeds, like those of dandelions, have tiny parachutes that allow them to float in the wind. Others, like burrs, have hooks that cling to animal fur, hitching a ride to new locations. Some plants even use explosive force to shoot their seeds like tiny rockets! These amazing methods of seed dispersal help plants grow in new places and ensure that forests, meadows, and gardens stay lush and full of life.

12. TORNADOES

The fastest winds on Earth are found in tornadoes. These powerful twisters can produce wind speeds of over 300 miles per hour! Tornadoes form during severe thunderstorms when warm, moist air meets cool, dry air, creating a rotating column of air. This spinning column can cause massive destruction, picking up cars, tearing off roofs, and uprooting trees.

13. OCEAN CURRENTS

Ocean currents are like rivers in the ocean, moving water around the world. They play a crucial role in regulating Earth's climate by distributing heat and nutrients. For example, the Gulf Stream brings warm water from the Gulf of Mexico to the North Atlantic.

14. HIBERNATION

Some animals, like bears and groundhogs, hibernate during the winter to conserve energy and survive harsh conditions.

During hibernation, their heart rate and metabolism slow down, and they sleep for long periods without eating.

15. PLANT PHOTOSYNTHESIS

Photosynthesis is the process by which plants make their own food using sunlight, water, and carbon dioxide. They absorb sunlight through their leaves and convert it into energy to grow and produce oxygen as a byproduct.

16. FOSSILS

Fossils are the preserved remains or traces of ancient plants and animals. They provide valuable clues about Earth's history and the evolution of life over millions of years. Fossils can be found in rocks, ice, and even amber.

17. BIOMES

A biome is a large geographic area with similar climate, vegetation, and animal life. Examples include deserts, grasslands, forests, and tundras. Each biome has its own unique characteristics and species adapted to its environment.

18. NATURAL WONDERS

From the Grand Canyon to the Great Barrier Reef, the world is full of breathtaking natural wonders. These awe-inspiring landscapes and ecosystems attract millions of visitors each year and inspire wonder and appreciation for nature's beauty.

19. ANIMAL COMMUNICATION

Animals communicate with each other in various ways, including sounds, body language, and scents. For example, whales sing complex songs to communicate with other members of their pod, and bees perform intricate dances to tell their hive mates where to find food.

20. RENEWABLE ENERGY

Did you know that the wind turbines you see on wind farms can generate enough electricity to power thousands of homes? Just one large wind turbine can produce over 1.5 million kilowatt-hours of electricity per year, which is enough to supply power to about 400 to 500 homes. Wind energy is a clean and renewable source of power that helps reduce our reliance on fossil fuels and decrease greenhouse gas emissions.

NATURE
EXPERT
QUIZZES

QUIZ 1: INCREDIBLE INSECTS

Question: Which insect can carry objects up to 50 times its own body weight?

A) Butterfly

B) Ant

C) Beetle

D) Dragonfly

Answer: B) Ant.

Ants are incredibly strong for their size and can lift and carry objects that are up to 50 times their own body weight. This strength helps them gather food, build nests, and protect their colonies. Some species of ants also work together to move even larger objects!

QUIZ 2: MARVELOUS MAMMALS

Question: Which mammal is capable of the longest migration?

A) African elephant

B) Humpback whale

C) Gray wolf

D) Arctic fox

Answer: B) Humpback whale.

Humpback whales are known for their incredible migrations, traveling up to 5,000 miles each way from their feeding grounds in polar regions to their breeding grounds in tropical waters. This long journey is one of the longest migrations of any mammal on Earth.

QUIZ 3: THE LARGEST LIVING ORGANISM

Question: What is the largest single living organism based on area?

A) Blue whale

B) Honey fungus

C) Giant sequoia tree

D) Posidonia australis seagrass

Answer: D) Posidonia australis seagrass.

The largest single living organism based on area is a specimen of Posidonia australis seagrass, also known as Poseidon's ribbon weed, located in Shark Bay off Western Australia. This enormous seagrass meadow covers approximately 200 square kilometers (77 square miles), which is equivalent to around 28,000 soccer fields or more than 450 times bigger than Vatican City, the world's smallest country. This vast seagrass meadow plays a crucial role in the marine ecosystem, providing habitat for many aquatic species and helping to stabilize the ocean floor.

QUIZ 4: DESERT WONDERS

Question: Which desert is the driest nonpolar desert on Earth?

A) Sahara Desert

B) Gobi Desert

C) Atacama Desert

D) Mojave Desert

Answer: C) Atacama Desert.

The Atacama Desert in Chile is the driest nonpolar desert on Earth. Some weather stations in the Atacama have never recorded any rainfall, and certain areas receive less than 0.04 inches (1 millimeter) of rain per year. Despite its extreme dryness, the Atacama is home to unique plants and animals adapted to its harsh conditions.

QUIZ 5: AMAZING AMPHIBIANS

Question: Which amphibian is known for its ability to regenerate lost body parts?

A) Frog

B) Toad

C) Salamander

D) Newt

Answer: C) Salamander.

Salamanders are amazing creatures that can regenerate lost body parts, such as tails, limbs, and even parts of their heart and brain. This incredible ability helps them recover from injuries and continue thriving in their environments.

QUIZ 6: OCEAN GIANTS

Question: Which marine animal is known for being the largest invertebrate?

A) Giant squid

B) Blue whale

C) Great white shark

D) Manta ray

Answer: A) Giant squid.

The giant squid is the largest invertebrate in the ocean, with some individuals reaching lengths of up to 43 feet. These elusive creatures live in deep ocean waters and are rarely seen by humans. They have large eyes to help them see in the dark depths of the ocean.

QUIZ 7: POLAR MARVELS

Question: Which animal can be found at the North Pole but not at the South Pole?

A) Penguin

B) Polar bear

C) Walrus

D) Seal

Answer: B) Polar bear.

Polar bears are native to the Arctic region and can be found at the North Pole. They are excellent swimmers and rely on sea ice to hunt for seals. Unlike polar bears, penguins live in the Southern Hemisphere, primarily in Antarctica.

QUIZ 8: FLYING MAMMALS

Question: Which mammal can glide through the air using flaps of skin?

A) Flying squirrel

B) Kangaroo

C) Raccoon

D) Hedgehog

Answer: A) Flying squirrel.

Flying squirrels have special flaps of skin called patagia that stretch from their wrists to their ankles. These flaps allow them to glide through the air from tree to tree, helping them escape predators and find food.

QUIZ 9: REMARKABLE RAINFORESTS

Question: What percentage of the Earth's species are found in rainforests?

A) 10%

B) 25%

C) 50%

D) 75%

Answer: C) 50%.

Rainforests are incredibly biodiverse and are home to about 50% of all the Earth's species, even though they cover only about 6% of the planet's surface. These lush ecosystems are vital for maintaining global biodiversity and supporting countless forms of life.

QUIZ 10: WONDERFUL WATERWAYS

Question: Which river is the longest in the world?

A) Amazon River

B) Nile River

C) Mississippi River

D) Yangtze River

Answer: B) Nile River.

The Nile River is the longest river in the world, stretching about 4,135 miles (6,650 kilometers) through northeastern Africa. It flows through eleven countries and is crucial for agriculture, transportation, and drinking water for millions of people living along its banks.

FACTS
BEYOND
EARTH

LOOKING AT THE STARS

 1 The **Sun** makes a sound, but we can't hear it.

 2 A **comet** smells like rotten eggs, urine, burning matches, and almonds.

 3 You can play **yo-yo** in space.

 4 Saturn can **float** on water.

 5 The **hottest** planet in our solar system is Venus.

6 **Mercury & Venus** are the only two planets in our solar system that have no moons.

 7 1.3 million Earths can fit inside the **Sun**.

LOOKING AT THE STARS

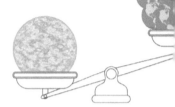

8 The **Sun** weighs about 330,000 times more than Earth.

9 A person who weighs 220 lbs on Earth would weigh 84 lbs on **Mars**.

10 As of today, Jupiter has **95 moons** that have been officially recognized by the International Astronomical Union.

11 The Sun makes a full rotation once every **25 – 35 days**.

12 Pluto is **smaller** than the United States.

13 There are more volcanoes on **Venus** than any other planet in our solar system.

14 **One year** on Uranus is roughly equal to 84 Earth years.

LOOKING AT THE STARS

15 Any free-moving liquid in outer space will form itself into a **sphere**.

16 Only 5% of the universe is **visible** from Earth.

17 Outer space is only **62 miles** away.

18 We always see the **same side** of the Moon, no matter where we stand on Earth.

19 On **Venus**, it snows metal and rains sulfuric acid.

20 The Moon is **moving away** from Earth at about 1.49 inches (3.78 centimeters) per year.

THINGS YOU MIGHT NOT KNOW ABOUT SPACE

1. THE BIG BANG

The universe began about 13.8 billion years ago in an event called the Big Bang. It started as a tiny, hot, dense point and has been expanding ever since. The Big Bang created everything in the universe, including galaxies, stars, planets, and even us!

2. GALAXIES

Our galaxy, the Milky Way, is just one of billions of galaxies in the universe. One of the coolest galaxies is the Andromeda Galaxy, our closest big neighbor. It's about 2.5 million light-years away and is on a collision course with the Milky Way! In about 4.5 billion years, the two galaxies will merge to form a new, larger galaxy. Don't worry, though—this cosmic dance won't affect us for a very, very long time!

3. BLACK HOLES

Black holes are regions of space where gravity is so strong that nothing, not even light, can escape. They form when massive stars collapse at the end of their life cycles. Black holes can be millions or even billions of times more massive than our Sun. There are probably millions of black holes in the Milky Way alone, orbiting like the stars, but we cannot see them.

4. BEST PLACE TO CELEBRATE BIRTHDAYS

A day on Mercury lasts longer than its year! Mercury zooms around the sun faster than any other planet, completing its year in just 88 Earth days. But guess what? A single day on Mercury—from one sunrise to the next— takes a whopping 176 Earth days! So, if you lived on Mercury, you'd celebrate two birthdays in just one very long day!

5. EARTH AND MOON DISTANCE

Did you know that all the planets in our Solar System can fit in the space between Earth and the Moon? If you lined up Mercury, Venus, Mars, Jupiter, Saturn, Uranus, and Neptune side by side, their combined diameters would fit within the 238,855 miles (384,400 kilometers) distance between Earth and the Moon. In fact, you'd still have about 2,729 miles (4,392 kilometers) of space left over!

6. DARK UNIVERSE

Did you know there are parts of the universe we can't see because their light hasn't reached us yet? The universe is so vast and has been expanding since the Big Bang, about 13.8 billion years ago. Even though light travels incredibly fast—about 186,282 miles per second—there are distant regions so far away that their light is still on its way to us. This means that the observable universe is just a small part of the entire cosmos.

7. THE JOURNEY OF A PHOTON

Did you know it takes a photon, which is a tiny particle of light, about 170,000 years to travel from the core of the Sun to its surface? The journey is like a giant game of pinball, with photons bouncing around in the Sun's dense layers. But once a photon finally reaches the surface, it zooms through space at the speed of light and takes just about eight minutes to reach Earth! So, the sunlight you see today started its journey inside the Sun long before humans even existed!

8. A COSMIC TIME MACHINE

Light takes time to travel across vast distances of space, and the stars and galaxies you see show you their light from years, centuries, or even millions of years ago. For example, the light from the closest star, Proxima Centauri, takes about 4.24 years to reach us, so we're seeing it as it was over four years ago. And when you look at the Andromeda Galaxy, you're seeing light that left it about 2.5 million years ago! This cosmic time travel makes stargazing like peering into a fascinating time machine.

9. FOREVER FOOTPRINT

On the Moon, footprints can last forever! That's because there's no wind or water to erode them. Unlike Earth, where weather and the atmosphere can quickly change the landscape, the Moon's surface is calm and frozen. This means that the footprints left by

astronauts during the Apollo missions will stay exactly where they are for millions of years!

10. STARS VS. SAND

There are more stars in the universe than grains of sand on all the beaches and deserts on Earth. Scientists estimate that our Milky Way galaxy alone contains about 100 billion stars. There are over 2 trillion galaxies in the observable universe, each with its own billions or even trillions of stars. When you add it all up, the number of stars reaches an unimaginable total of around 1 septillion (that's a 1 followed by 24 zeros!). So next time you see a handful of sand, imagine countless more stars shining across the cosmos!

11. ROGUE PLANETS

There are rogue planets drifting through the universe, not orbiting any star. These lonely planets have been knocked out of their original orbits and now wander through space. Because they don't have a star to light them up, spotting them is incredibly difficult. Scientists believe there could be many of these rogue planets, but we don't know if any are close to our Solar

System. These cosmic drifters could potentially collide with other planets or even join new star systems on their endless journey through the cosmos!

12. COMETS

Comets are like giant dirty snowballs from outer space, made of ice, dust, and rock. One of the most famous comets is Halley's Comet. It is consistently visible to the naked eye from Earth, appearing every 75-79 years. The last time it passed by was in 1986, and it will be back again in 2061. When a comet gets close to the Sun, it heats up and starts to glow, creating a beautiful, bright tail that can stretch for millions of miles across the sky.

13. ASTEROIDS

Asteroids are rocky objects that orbit the Sun, and one of the most famous asteroids is called Ceres. Ceres is so big that it's classified as a dwarf planet! It's located in the asteroid belt between Mars and Jupiter and makes up about one-third of the entire mass of the asteroid belt. Scientists believe that Ceres might even have water ice beneath its surface, making it an exciting object to study in space.

14. PLANETARY RINGS

Saturn is famous for its stunning rings, which are made up of billions of ice and rock particles. But did you know that the rings are so wide they could fit about six Earths lined up in a row? Despite their enormous width, the rings are surprisingly thin, often only about 30 feet thick! These dazzling rings reflect sunlight, making Saturn one of the most beautiful planets to observe through a telescope.

15. THE MOON

The Moon is Earth's only natural satellite and the fifth-largest moon in the solar system. It's about 238,900 miles away from Earth and takes about 27.3 days to orbit us. The moon's gravitational pull causes tides on Earth.

16. LARGEST STAR

The largest known star in the universe is UY Scuti. It's a red supergiant star located in the Milky Way galaxy, about 9,500 light-years from Earth. UY Scuti is so huge that if it were placed in the center of our Solar System, it would reach beyond the orbit of Jupiter! This giant star is over 1,700 times wider than our Sun, making it a truly colossal object in the universe.

17. MILLIONS OF STARS. OR THOUSANDS?

Even though there are billions of stars in our Milky Way galaxy, you cannot see millions of stars at night with just your eyes. On a clear, dark night away from city lights, you can see about 2,000 to 3,000 stars. Each of these stars is like a distant sun, and some might even have their own planets orbiting them. Imagine all the amazing things that could be out there in the universe!

18. THE SPEED OF LIGHT

The speed of light is about 186,282 miles per second (299,792 kilometers per second). Light travels incredibly fast and is the quickest thing in the universe. It takes about 8 minutes for sunlight to reach Earth from the Sun.

19. NEUTRON STARS

Neutron stars are some of the most fascinating objects in the universe. They are the remnants of massive stars that have exploded in supernovas. Despite being only about 12 miles in diameter, they are incredibly dense. Just a teaspoon of neutron star material would weigh about 6 billion tons on Earth! These cosmic heavyweights also spin very rapidly, sometimes hundreds of times per second, creating beams of light that can be seen as pulsars.

20. THE LARGEST RADIO GALAXY

Did you know that the Alcyoneus Galaxy is one of the largest known radio galaxies in the universe? It's a staggering 16 million light-years across, making it about 160 times larger than the Milky Way! This colossal galaxy emits powerful radio waves from its massive jets of charged particles, stretching far beyond its visible boundaries.

COSMIC TRIVIA FOR GENIUSES

QUIZ 1: THE SOLAR SYSTEM

Question: What is the center of our Solar System?

A) Earth

B) Moon

C) Sun

D) Mars

Answer: C) Sun.

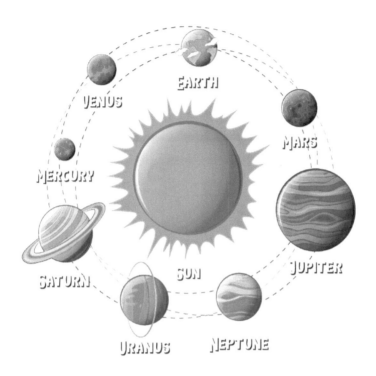

The Sun is at the center of our Solar System. It is a huge, glowing ball of hot gases that provides light and heat to all the planets, including Earth. Without the Sun, we wouldn't have daytime, and life on Earth wouldn't be possible. It helps plants grow, warms our planet, and even gives us beautiful sunrises and sunsets.

QUIZ 2: PLANETS

Question: Which planet is known as the "Red Planet"?

A) Venus

B) Jupiter

C) Mars

D) Saturn

Answer: C) Mars.

Mars is called the "Red Planet" because its surface is covered with iron oxide, which makes it look red. It's the fourth planet from the Sun and has the largest volcano and canyon in the entire Solar System. Scientists are very interested in Mars because it might have had water on its surface long ago.

QUIZ 3: COSMIC DUST

Question: What constantly falls onto Earth from space, covering it with tiny particles?

A) Cosmic dust

B) Meteorites

C) Starlight

D) Solar flares

Answer: A) Cosmic dust.

Cosmic dust constantly falls onto Earth from space, covering it with tiny particles. This dust comes from comets, asteroids, and other celestial bodies and enters our atmosphere, where it slowly settles on the ground. Every year, Earth accumulates thousands of tons of this cosmic dust, which contributes to our understanding of the solar system and the universe. These tiny particles are so small that we don't notice them, but they are all around us.

QUIZ 4: STARS

Question: What is a group of stars that forms a pattern in the sky called?

A) Galaxy

B) Comet

C) Constellation

D) Nebula

Answer: C) Constellation.

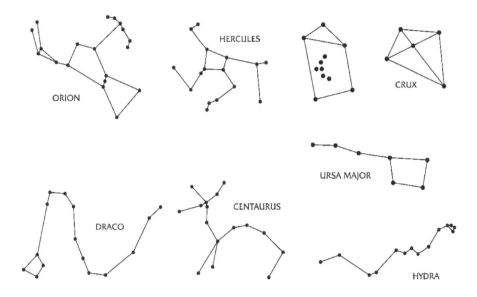

A constellation is a group of stars that forms a pattern or picture in the sky. These patterns often look like animals, mythological figures, or objects. For example, Orion looks like a hunter, and Ursa Major looks like a big bear. People have used constellations for navigation and storytelling for thousands of years.

QUIZ 5: GALAXIES

Question: What is the name of the galaxy we live in?

A) Andromeda Galaxy

B) Milky Way Galaxy

C) Whirlpool Galaxy

D) Sombrero Galaxy

Answer: B) Milky Way Galaxy.

We live in the Milky Way Galaxy, which is a spiral galaxy with billions of stars, including our Sun. It looks like a milky band of light stretching across the sky. Our Solar System is in one of the spiral arms of the Milky Way, and it's just one of many galaxies in the universe.

QUIZ 6: TRAVELING TO THE NEAREST STAR

Question: How long would it take to drive a car to the nearest star, Proxima Centauri, at 70 mph?

A) 1 million years

B) 10 million years

C) 1 billion years

D) More than 356 billion years

Answer: D) More than 356 billion years.

If you could drive a car at 70 mph to the nearest star, Proxima Centauri, it would take more than 356 billion years to get there! Proxima Centauri is about 4.24 light-years away from Earth, and light travels at an incredible speed of about 186,282 miles per second. Driving a car, even at highway speeds, is incredibly slow compared to the vast distances in space.

QUIZ 7: MOON PHASES

Question: How bright is the Moon during its First and Last Quarter phases compared to when it is Full?

A) 50 percent as bright

B) 25 percent as bright

C) 10 percent as bright

D) 75 percent as bright

Answer: C) 10 percent as bright.

When the Moon is in its First and Last Quarter phases, it appears half-full, but it is only 10 percent as bright as the Full Moon. This is because the angle at which the sunlight hits the Moon and reflects back to Earth is less direct during these phases, resulting in less overall brightness. The Full Moon, on the other hand, is fully illuminated by the Sun, making it much brighter.

QUIZ 8: JOURNEY THROUGH EARTH

Question: If you drilled a tunnel through Earth and jumped in, how long would it take to reach the other side?

A) 30 minutes

B) 42 minutes and 12 seconds

C) 1 hour

D) 50 minutes

Answer: B) 42 minutes and 12 seconds.

If you drilled a tunnel straight through Earth and jumped in, it would take approximately 42 minutes and 12 seconds to reach the other side. This time is calculated based on the force of gravity accelerating you towards the Earth's center and then decelerating you as you move towards the other side. This hypothetical journey illustrates the fascinating effects of gravity and Earth's structure.

QUIZ 9: MOON ORBITS

Question: How long does it take for the Moon to orbit the Earth?

A) 7 days

B) 14 days

C) 27.3 days

D) 365 days

Answer: C) 27.3 days.

It takes the Moon approximately 27.3 days to complete one orbit around the Earth. This period is known as a sidereal month. During this time, we see the Moon go through its phases, from the new Moon to the full Moon and back again. This regular orbit is why we experience consistent lunar phases and why the Moon's appearance changes in the sky over the course of a month.

QUIZ 10: SPACE TELESCOPES

Question: What is the name of the famous space telescope that orbits Earth and takes pictures of distant galaxies and stars?

A) Hubble Space Telescope

B) James Webb Telescope

C) Kepler Space Telescope

D) Galileo Telescope

Answer: A) Hubble Space Telescope.

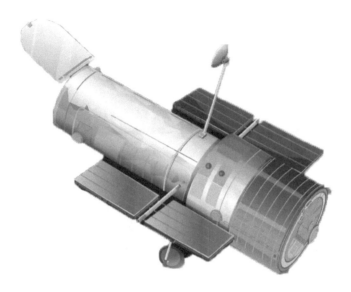

The Hubble Space Telescope is a famous telescope that orbits Earth. It has taken amazing pictures of galaxies, stars, and other cosmic objects since it was launched in 1990. Hubble's discoveries have helped scientists learn a lot about the universe, including how fast it is expanding and the age of distant stars.

SCAVENGER HUNT

SCAVENGER HUNT

1. What was the Great Pyramid of Giza's original height? Hint: section Hidden Gems of History, fact number 1.

2. What percentage of the world's freshwater do glaciers store?

Hint: section Unveiling Earth's Mysteries, fact number 19.

3. How hot can a single bolt of lightning heat the air around it?

Hint: section A Feast of Science Facts, fact number 1.

4. Why do footprints on the Moon last forever?

Hint: section Things You Might Not Know About Space, fact number 9.

5. What caused the Black Death in the 14th century?

Hint: section Hidden Gems of History, fact number 5.

6. Where is the tallest waterfall in the world located?

Hint: section Unveiling Earth's Mysteries, fact number 4.

7. What rare phenomenon occurs at night and is created by the light of the moon?

Hint: section A Feast of Science Facts, fact number 3.

8. What causes Earth's seasons?

Hint: section Unveiling Earth's Mysteries, fact number 16.

9. How long does it take for a photon to travel from the core of the Sun to its surface, and then to Earth?

Hint: section Things You Might Not Know About Space, fact number 7.

10. How fast does Earth spin at the equator?

Hint: section A Feast of Science Facts, fact number 8.

11. Why are there parts of the universe we can't see?

Hint: section Things You Might Not Know About Space, fact number 6.

12. How fast can bamboo grow in a single day?

Hint: section A Feast of Science Facts, fact number 16.

13. How long is the Great Wall of China?

Hint: section Hidden Gems of History, fact number 7.

14. How old is Earth?

Hint: section Unveiling Earth's Mysteries, fact number 1.

15. Why do stars appear to twinkle when viewed from Earth?

Hint: section A Feast of Science Facts, fact number 19.

16. Where is the Great Blue Hole?

Hint: section Unveiling Earth's Mysteries, fact number 15.

17. Which sea creature can change its shape, color, and behavior to imitate other sea creatures?

Hint: section Epic Encounters with Nature, fact number 3.

18. What allows geckos to walk on walls and even upside down?

Hint: section A Feast of Science Facts, fact number 4.

19. How long does a day on Mercury last compared to its year?

Hint: section Things You Might Not Know About Space, fact number 4.

20. How many active volcanoes are there on Earth?

Hint: section Unveiling Earth's Mysteries, fact number 12.

21. How do Arctic foxes adapt their fur color to the seasons?

Hint: section Epic Encounters with Nature, fact number 9.

22. What is the oldest known living organism, and how old can it be?

Hint: section A Feast of Science Facts, fact number 15.

23. What is the largest hot desert in the world?

Hint: section Unveiling Earth's Mysteries, fact number 6.

24. What is the name of our closest big neighboring galaxy, and how far is it from us?

Hint: section Things You Might Not Know About Space, fact number 2.

25. How much energy does the Sun produce every second?

Hint: section A Feast of Science Facts, fact number 10.

26. What is the name of the oldest known tree in the world?

Hint: section Unveiling Earth's Mysteries, fact number 11.

27. What percentage of the world's oxygen is produced by the Amazon Rainforest?

Hint: section Epic Encounters with Nature, fact number 7.

28. What layer of Earth's atmosphere do humans live in?

Hint: section Unveiling Earth's Mysteries, fact number 7.

29. What special gland do penguins have that helps them drink seawater?

Hint: section A Feast of Science Facts, fact number 14.

30. How high can sand dunes in the Sahara Desert reach?

Hint: section Unveiling Earth's Mysteries, fact number 20.

ANSWER SHEET

1. 481 feet tall.

2. They store about 69% of the world's fresh water.

3. Up to 50,000 degrees Fahrenheit.

4. Because there's no wind or water to erode them.

5. Fleas on rats.

6. Venezuela (Angel Falls).

7. Moonbows.

8. Earth's tilt on its axis.

9. About 170,000 years to travel from the core to the surface, and about eight minutes to reach Earth.

10. About 1,000 miles per hour.

11. Because their light hasn't reached us yet.

12. Up to 35 inches.

13. Over 13,000 miles.

14. About 4.5 billion years old.

15. Because their light passes through Earth's atmosphere, which bends the light.

16. Off the coast of Belize.

17. The mimic octopus.

18. Millions of tiny hairs on their feet called setae.

19. A day on Mercury lasts 176 Earth days, while its year lasts 88 Earth days.

20. About 1,500.

21. Their fur turns white in winter and brown or gray in summer.

22. A type of sea sponge called the glass sponge, over 10,000 years old.

23. The Sahara Desert.

24. The Andromeda Galaxy, about 2.5 million light-years away.

25. Enough to power the entire Earth for 500,000 years.

26. Methuselah (a Bristlecone Pine).

27. About 20%.

28. The troposphere.

29. A gland above their eyes that removes salt from the seawater.

30. Up to 600 feet.

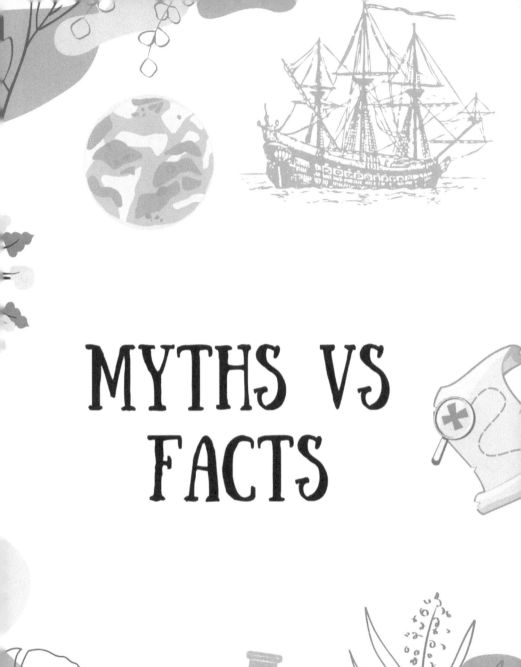

MYTHS VS FACTS

MYTHS OR FACTS?

1. Water conducts electricity.

2. The Moon has a dark side.

3. The Great Wall of China is the only man-made structure you can see from the Moon.

4. Goldfish have three-second memories.

5. Sea turtles use Earth's magnetic field to navigate.

6. Milk helps you grow big and tall and strong.

7. Going outside with wet hair can give you a cold.

8. Fire and lava only burn you if they touch you.

9. A T-rex can still see you even if you stay perfectly still.

10. The Sun's color is white.

11. Bats are blind.

12. Bees die after they sting you.

13. You can rescue a baby bird and put it back in its nest without causing the parent to abandon it.

14. Porcupines cannot shoot their quills.

15. Mountains often form under the sea.

16. Trees provide the air we breathe.

17. A tree grows one ring per year.

18. The Earth is a perfect sphere.

19. Sloths are good at swimming.

20. Ants can be found on every single continent except Antarctica.

ANSWER SHEET

1. Myth.

   Pure water doesn't conduct electricity; it's the impurities in water, like salts and minerals, that do.

2. Myth.

   Both sides of the moon receive sunlight. People call it the "dark side" because it's always facing away from Earth and we never see it, but it's not actually dark.

3. Myth.

   No man-made structures, including the Great Wall of China, are visible from the Moon without aid. Even though the wall is very long, it is also very thin, making it essentially invisible.

4. Myth.

   Goldfish have much longer memories, capable of remembering things for months. They can be trained to recognize sounds, colors, and even perform tricks.

5. Fact.

6. Myth.

While milk contains important nutrients like calcium and vitamin D, it's not the only factor in growing big and tall. A balanced diet, genetics, and overall health also play crucial roles in growth and strength.

7. Myth.

Colds are caused by viruses, not by being cold or having wet hair. Going outside with wet hair might make you feel chilly, but it won't cause you to catch a cold.

8. Myth.

Fire and lava can burn you even if they don't touch you directly, due to the intense heat they radiate. Being close to them can cause severe burns from the radiant heat alone.

9. Fact.

10. Fact.

11. Myth.

Bats are not blind; they have eyes and can see. Many bats use echolocation to navigate in the dark, but they also rely on their vision, especially in low light conditions.

12. Partly fact.

This is true for honeybees, which have barbed stingers that get stuck in the skin, leading to their death after stinging. However, other bee species, like bumblebees and wasps, can sting multiple times without dying.

13. Fact.

14. Fact.

15. Fact.

16. Myth.

Trees produce oxygen through photosynthesis, which is vital for the air we breathe. However, oceans and other plants also contribute significantly to the Earth's oxygen supply.

17. Myth.

In temperate regions, trees produce two rings per year: a wider, lighter ring during spring and a narrower, darker ring in autumn. This creates a clear separation that allows us to distinguish each year's growth. However, in tropical climates, where there are no distinct seasons, trees may not show visible rings.

18. Myth.

The Earth is not a perfect sphere; it is an oblate spheroid. This means it is slightly flattened at the poles and bulging at the equator due to its rotation.

19. Fact.

20. Fact.

SOMETHING FOR YOU

Hey there, Amazing Reader!

Wow! We've come to the end of our fun adventure through incredible facts, mind-blowing trivia, and jaw-dropping discoveries!

Thank you so much for joining me on this journey! You've been an awesome explorer, and I hope you had as much fun reading these facts as I did sharing them with you.

Keep asking questions and exploring the world around you—there's always something new to discover!

FREE BONUSES

Scan the QR code below to unlock awesome bonuses!

Made in United States
Troutdale, OR
10/03/2024

23361239R00106